*Blood Gold* is about how gold discoveries in Australia created an unprecedented population explosion and with it came crime and lawlessness.

**READ** about law and order on the goldfields and how gold was a target for theft.

**LEARN** how the Native Police were used to enforce law and order.

**FIND OUT** about the expanding frontier and how the Native Police were used to "disperse" First Nations people from their lands to make way for colonisation.

**DISCOVER** Australia's first Chinese bushranger, and

**READ** about some of Australia's female bushrangers

and much more…

Gold! Hidden Stories of Australia's Past, Book 5

# Blood Gold

## Native Police, Bushrangers, and Law and Order on the Goldfields

## Marji Hill

Published by The Prison Tree Press 2022

Copyright © 2022 Marji Hill

Copyright © 2022 Artwork and paintings by Marji Hill

Editor: Eddie Dowd

Cover - "Punitive Expedition" 5'x6' oil painting by Marji Hill

ISBN  978-0-6454834-8-2  paperback
ISBN  978-0-6454834-9-9  eBook

 A catalogue record for this work is available from the National Library of Australia

The Prison Tree Press - Suite 124, 1-10 Albert Avenue, Broadbeach, Qld, 4218
https://marjihill.com
https://www.fastselfpublishing.com

All rights reserved. No part of this book may be reproduced, stored in a retrieval system, or transmitted in any form or by any means, electronic, mechanical, photocopying, recording, scanning, or otherwise, without the prior written permission of the publisher.

Disclaimer:

All the material contained in this book is provided for educational and informational purposes only. No responsibility can be taken for any results or outcomes resulting from the use of this material.

While every care has been taken to trace and acknowledge copyright the publishers tender their apologies for any accidental infringement where copyright has proved untraceable.

Every attempt has been made to provide information that is both accurate and effective, however, the author does not assume any responsibility for the accuracy or use/misuse of this information.

WARNING: Aboriginal and Torres Strait Islander people are advised that this book contains images and names of people who have passed away.

# THE SERIES

## Gold! Hidden Stories of Australia's Past

### Book 1
*The Gates of Gold*:
The Discovery of Gold, its Legacy and its Contribution to Australian Identity

### Book 2
*Shadows of Gold*:
Eureka and the Birth of Australian democracy

### Book 3
*Gold and the Chinese*:
Racism, Riots and Protest on the Australian Goldfields

### Book 4
*Ghosts of Gold*:
The Life and Times of Jupiter Mosman

### Book 5
*Blood Gold*:
Native Police, Bushrangers and Law and Order on the Goldfields

# DEDICATION

To

John Joseph Foley

# TABLE OF CONTENTS

Chapter 1 — Lawlessness on the Goldfields ..............................1

Chapter 2 — Law Enforcement and Protection........................17

Chapter 3 — Native Police ................................................................31

Chapter 4 — The Queensland Frontier .......................................47

Chapter 5 — Bushrangers ................................................................61

Chapter 6 — Sam Poo .......................................................................75

Chapter 7 — Mary Ann Bugg..........................................................83

SOURCES ............................................................................................103

About Marji Hill.................................................................................113

More Books by Marji Hill ...............................................................119

# ACKNOWLEDGEMENTS

I acknowledge the Traditional Custodians of Country throughout Australia and their connections to land, sea, and community. I pay my respects to elders, past, present, and emerging and extend my respects to all First Nations peoples today.

In the spirit of reconciliation, my mission is to increase understanding between the First Nations and other Australians and to provide people from all over the globe some basic understanding of Australia's first people, their history, and cultures.

In my life I've been fortunate to have had several mentors. Alex Barlow, my late partner, would always say to me "If you manage your time well, you can achieve everything you want in life." That started my quest into the world of time management and learning how to maximise my productivity.

John Foley, barrister, helped me to expand my vision and has inspired me to make possible what seemed impossible. Sherien Foley has always been there to challenge and kickstart me and I remember her words when I hit rock bottom with my work many years ago and she said to me "There's only one way to go and that's up!"

This current series of books about gold grew out of a brainstorming session I had with my old friend, Gail Parr, while staying with her and her husband, George Sansbury at

Maryborough in Queensland. We thrashed out the concept and from this grew these five books.

I would also like to acknowledge the late and great Jim Lynch who introduced me to the Charters Towers gold story many years ago and to his, son, Mark Lynch, Chairperson of the Citigold Corporation, who has always supported and encouraged my creativity in books and in art.in relation to the gold story.

And finally, thank you Eddie Dowd, my backstop, mentor and helper in getting my books into their final form for publication.

**Marji Hill**

"As the discovery of gold created a population explosion and a wealthy, liberal society, the course of Australian history
was changed."
*Marji Hill*

# Chapter 1 – Lawlessness on the Goldfields

A legacy of the gold discoveries in Australia was crime and lawlessness.

With the discovery of gold in 1851 thousands of frenzied migrants packed up their families and belongings, left their home countries, boarded ships, and took the long and dangerous journey to the other side of the world. They descended onto the goldfields spurred on by the hope of becoming rich and prosperous.

In New South Wales (NSW) an exodus from Sydney headed to the goldfields. Likewise, in Victoria as rich goldfields were found gold-seekers arrived in their masses.

Gripped by gold fever men and women tried their luck on the goldfields dreaming of a better life for themselves and their families.

Australia was the destination and by the end of 1851 ships were on their way to down under laden with men and women from England, Scotland, Wales, and Ireland and others coming from Europe, the United States and China.

As the discovery of gold created a population explosion and a wealthy, liberal society the course of Australian history was changed.

On Wathaurung land, the epicentre for gold was Ballarat in Victoria which became the setting for one of the most dramatic episodes of all the great gold rushes - the Eureka rebellion.

In a confined space of a few hundred metres armies of prospectors went to work digging for gold. The lure of gold offered hope for a future life of prosperity.

The countryside was pockmarked with mining claims and while for some there was a bonanza as miners discovered huge quantities of gold for others there were claims that produced no gold at all.

## Crime on the goldfields

As desperate diggers flooded the goldfields there was a huge increase in crime.

Gold attracted all kinds of people. There were ex-convicts who had been transported to Australia for breaking the law in Britain. There were petty thieves; there were bushrangers; and there were swindlers.

Gold was a target for theft.

In was during the gold rushes that bushranging gained momentum. The legendary bushranger became part of the Australian identity.

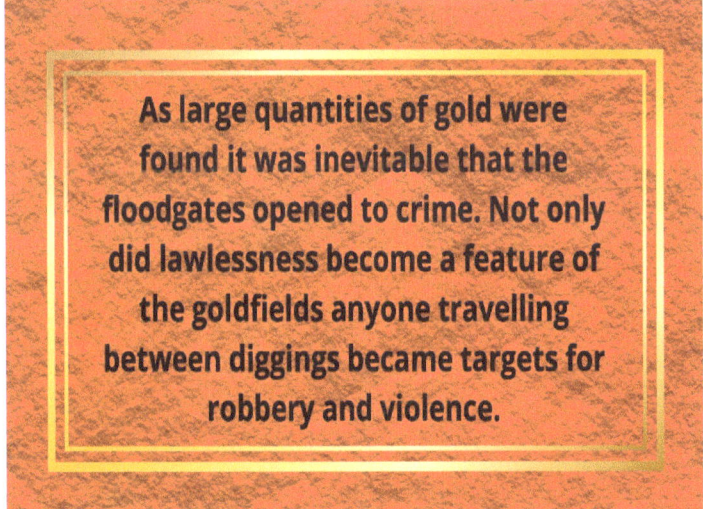

As large quantities of gold were found it was inevitable that the floodgates opened to crime. Not only did lawlessness become a feature of the goldfields anyone travelling between diggings became targets for robbery and violence.

As large quantities of gold were found it was inevitable that the floodgates opened to crime.

Not only did lawlessness become a feature of the goldfields but also anyone travelling between diggings became targets for robbery and violence.

Life was tough on the goldfields. Living conditions were cramped and rough. With people living in tents and shanties there were few comforts.

Tensions surfaced and fights broke out.

There were robberies and in the midst of huge wealth, there was also poverty, most of it extreme and easily traced back to the authorities as its source.

The goldfields were dangerous places.

In the multicultural melting pot of the Ballarat goldfield, there was plenty of rivalry and fighting.

Racism was rife and anti-Chinese sentiment grew.

## Alcohol

Alcohol was a prominent feature of life on the goldfields. Water was heavily polluted and drinking it was dangerous so it was inevitable that many miners turned to alcohol as their drink of choice[1].

Grog stimulated violence with drunken brawls becoming a common occurrence. It generated an unregulated and unsupervised trade in alcohol that led to crime and corruption.

The colonial government made it unlawful to make or sell liquor but this policy of prohibition was not effective.

Penalties were harsh for anyone making or selling alcohol on the goldfields. Police would issue heavy fines or, given the opportunity, they would overstep their mark. There were cases when police would resort to viciously

---

[1] Sovereign Hill Education Blog (2014) "Alcohol on the Goldfields" https://sovereignhilledblog.com/2014/02/21/alcohol-on-the-goldfields/

torching the tents of liquor sellers, destroying their possessions and seizing illegal alcohol[2].

## Claim jumping

Gold mining claims were often very small. If you wanted more land to mine you had to get another licence.

If you wanted to get gold that was not yours, claim jumping was common.

A claim had to be worked at least for a few hours a day. If it was not worked for twenty-four hours it could be taken over by someone else[3] and this led to violent arguments.

There was an underground version of claim jumping which involved digging in a neighbouring claim.

If a hard working miner had a sterile claim and tried to switch to another, his neighbours

---

[2] http://ergo.slv.vic.gov.au/explore-history/golden-victoria/life-fields/law-order
[3] Korzelinski, S. (1979) *Memoirs of Gold Digging in Australia*. St Lucia, Qld, University of Queensland Press, p 44

could jump either to his old one or the new one because he was not permitted two.

If there was a dispute the Gold Commissioner assisted by four assessors from among the miners was meant to adjudicate but with the rivalry and tensions of the time many disputes were resolved by the pick or the gun, or the threat of them[4].

## Theft of gold

Gold has always been a target for thieves so right from the beginning of the gold rush days gold was stolen.

Miners needed to keep their gold safe from bushrangers and thieves. To protect it some would bury it or hide it somewhere in a secret spot.

But usually, thieves knew where to start looking.

Some miners would leave a person behind at the tent to protect their gold; others used

---

[4] Grassby, Al and Hill, Marji(1988) *Six Australian Battlefields.* North Ryde, NSW, Angus & Robertson, p. 209.

guard dogs. Then some handed over their gold to the Gold Commissioner to transport it to cities.

If miners transported their gold themselves they were always in danger of either losing it or losing their claim.

There was a very real threat from bushrangers who terrorised travellers, ambushed them, and stole their gold. Regular gold transports attracted the attention of these highway thieves.

While every effort was made to protect the gold, there were no guarantees that it would ever be delivered safely. If a Gold Escort was held up and robbed, the owners of the gold could lose the lot.

## Bushranging

In this new society dominated by gold, bushranging was on the rise.

There were no banks in the early days. Miners who found gold had to keep it with them or transport it in Gold Escorts to the cities.

Gold was an attraction for bushrangers who were either petty thieves or cold-blooded bandits. In those gold rush years from 1851 to 1880 bushranging reached its height.

They were usually wild young men who took it up to get rich quick or to glory in notoriety. They were expert horsemen and given their thorough knowledge of the bush, they could easily outrun the law.

### Digger hunts

With all the great new wealth on the goldfields, the colonial authorities decided to capitalise on this. Lieutenant-Governor La Trobe introduced the Gold Licence which in turn bred anger, trouble, and discontent on the goldfields.

To ensure that the miners paid this tax, La Trobe ordered regular digger hunts. Soldiers and police were sent onto the goldfields to check for licences. A passing trooper might demand to view a licence when a miner was deep underground. It meant the miner had to climb possibly over 30 metres (100 feet) up a ladder to show the licence to the trooper. This inconvenience and interruption were annoying and time consuming[5].

The colonial administration put most of its energy into enforcing this unpopular gold licence, and in doing so, it neglected to control crime.

## Racial violence

The lawlessness on the goldfields included racial violence against the Chinese miners.

As soon as thousands of Chinese miners joined the other gold-seekers from around the world, anti-Chinese sentiment grew.

European diggers regarded the Chinese as aliens. Because Chinese mining methods were

---

[5] Sovereign Hill
https://sovereignhill.com.au/uploads/resources/SovHill-lawandorder-notes-ss1.pdf

very efficient and different, the Europeans feared an "invasion" of Chinese miners and were frightened that this competition would take too much of their gold.

The Chinese miners faced institutionalised discrimination and daily racism from the beginning of those early years.

Chinese miners were bullied and harassed. In 1854, a group of Chinese who had arrived at Melbourne wharf were beaten and abused.

Anti-Chinese violence included bashings, name calling, cruel practical jokes, scalping, harassment, theft and property destruction.

This anti-Chinese activity was commonplace among small groups of Europeans which broke out in all the gold mining towns like Bendigo, Castlemaine, Ballarat and others.

Where claim-jumping was considered the worst of poor form, in the European community violence against the Chinese miners was almost encouraged. This left the

Chinese vulnerable and exposed to theft and attack[6].

## Vigilante justice

It was common for miners on the goldfields to take the law into their own hands. "Protection committees" were set up and so often their punishments were brutal.

There were reports of thieves being flogged or chained to trees for days at a time. There were near lynchings, maiming, and even killings of those who committed crimes[7].

## Lawlessness

Given the degree of crime and lawlessness on the goldfields, many complained bitterly. Armed robberies and violence were common,

---

[6] Victorian Collections "Many Roads: Stories of the Chinese on the goldfields" https://victoriancollections.net.au/stories/many-roads-stories-of-the-chinese-on-the-goldfields/conflict-harmony
[7] SBS "Lawless and Disorderly" https://www.sbs.com.au/gold/lawless-and-disorderly/

and the newspapers were filled with reports of murder.

There was the instance of a boy being left to drown in a creek. Horses were stolen on a daily basis, and night stores were held up. Robberies and drunkenness were routine and there was thieving from tent dwellings.

The problem of lawlessness and crime on the goldfields was made worse by a drastic shortage of police in the early days of the gold rush. In July 1851, all but two of Melbourne's forty police resigned and took off to the goldfields.

Violence was even greater for First Nations peoples. Violence and murder against them during the gold rush period was extensive[8]. There was sexual abuse, and poisoning, their dogs were shot, and graves were desecrated but crimes against First Nations peoples were rarely prosecuted.

There was considerable fear for public order.

---

[8] https://www.jstor.org/stable/j.ctt24hcsc.13?seq=1

There was not much law and order and this lack of attention to crime on the part of the colonial authorities led to increased calls for law enforcement and police protection.

"The goldfields were dangerous places and with the lack of policing of actual crime, law and order were seriously defective."

*Marji Hill*

## Chapter 2 – Law Enforcement and Protection

In those early days of the gold rush miners were a good distance from any formal government infrastructure.

Melbourne at the time had a shortage of police and only a handful of soldiers. There had been a small contingent of police. Out of 40 in July 1851 all had resigned but two. The others took off to the goldfields[9].

These policemen needed to be replaced but recruiting suitable men for the police force was difficult. In this era, everyone was wanting to go to the goldfields to make their fortune.

As most of the European police had gone prospecting, Lieutenant-Governor Latrobe's

---

[9] Caitlin Mahar "Police"
https://www.egold.net.au/biogs/EG00187b.htm

only option was to send a small contingent of Native Police to the goldfields.

> **FIRST LAW ENFORCERS**
>
> The Native Police Corps were the first law enforcers on the goldfields. Their role was an important one in the discovery of gold and early government regulation of the Victorian goldfields.

The Native Police Corps were the first law enforcers on the goldfields.

Their role was an important one in the discovery of gold and early government regulation by the Victorian government.

However, there were not enough Native Police to cope with the growing needs of goldfields so more effort was put into police recruitment. In a desperate effort to grow the police force, police wages were increased and they took any application.

As a result, the police force was attracting the wrong type of recruits. They were either too old, too ill, or were failures at what they did. Some were simply too desperate to work. Ex-convicts, ex-wardens and military pensioners from Van Diemen's Land were being recruited. Given their backgrounds, these types were prone to brutality, corruption, and violence.

## Administering the goldfields

With the population on the Victorian goldfields rapidly growing, the government appointed commissioners and a contingent of police to administer them. This was based on the New South Wales (NSW) model so each goldfield had a

- Commissioner,
- Assistant Commissioner
- Clerk

- Inspector of Police, and
- A detachment of Troopers (mounted police) and foot police.

They were to maintain law and order on the goldfields. Apart from settling disputes over claims they had to supervise the collection, storage and transportation of gold.

They also had to manage the gold licence system. They had to issue the licences, collect the fees, and fine those who did not comply.

The quality of the police on the goldfields and the incentives they were given to find miners without licences became a source of frustration and discontent on the goldfields[10].

## Gold Escorts

Early in the gold rush days if gold had to be sent to Melbourne it was sent with the mail run. It was not long, however, that the mail

---

[10] Sovereign Hill (2014) https://sovereignhilledblog.com/2014/03/20/the-goldfields-police/

run didn't have sufficient capacity to carry larger quantities of gold. This service also became too dangerous.

Miners who wanted to take their gold to Sydney, Melbourne or Adelaide for safekeeping, risked being "bailed up" by bushrangers if they took it themselves. There was also the risk of theft if it was sent by coach.

Carrying gold in large quantities was a risky exercise.

Police troopers became escorts for these mail coaches. Even then, bushrangers could not resist the lure of so much wealth in one place which was being transported through wild bush country.

Gold Escorts were established to safely carry the gold.

In September 1851 the first Gold Escort went from Ballarat to Melbourne's Treasury and to Geelong. It was heavily guarded by armed mounted police, two troopers, two Native Police and the Gold Commissioner[11].

They were a target for bushrangers.

Miners would pay a fee for the service. If they wanted to send their gold to the cities for safekeeping the gold was handed to the gold commissioner. The gold was then weighed, a receipt was given, and it was put into a sealed pouch with the receipt attached to it. A copy of the receipt was given to each miner.

When the miners got to the city, they handed this receipt to officials at the Treasury. After showing their receipt, describing the gold, and proving their identity, the miners got back their gold[12].

Eventually, enterprising business people established private escort companies to take over the role of transporting gold to the cities.

---

[11] Electronic Encyclopedia of Gold in Australia "A nation's heritage" https://www.egold.net.au/biogs/EG00143b.htm
[12] Webber, Kimberley (2001) *Law and Order on the Goldfields.* South Yarra, Vic, Macmillan, p. 13

## Gold licence

In August 1851 La Trobe followed the lead taken by NSW and announced a monthly licence tax of thirty shillings.

The colonial authorities wanted to capitalise on miners finding gold so they decided to tax miners and others working on the goldfields for revenue. Not only the miners but anyone working on the goldfields had to get a gold licence.

This applied to anyone who had a business, operated as a tradesman, or was engaged in other occupations on the goldfields.

The introduction of the gold licence resulted in a lot of anger, trouble, hostility and outrage. There were protest meetings not only in Ballarat but at Bendigo, Castlemaine and also Melbourne.

The miners felt that they had a right to be consulted about the tax. Discontent flared up. This ill feeling amongst the thousands of miners on the goldfields was what would ultimately lead to the Eureka Rebellion.

The gold licence was a way of putting the brake on so many people leaving their places of work in the cities and going to the goldfields.

Paying a licence fee to the government meant miners could dig for gold in a specific area of ground. At the end of each month the miners had to pay the fee again and get another licence.

Even if diggers were unsuccessful at finding gold they still had to pay the gold tax.

Expenses were high.

Police had to regulate the goldfields, sell the licences, and check that the miners had their licences.

If you couldn't produce your licence you were arrested and fined.

This checking of licences became the priority for the police.

The Gold Commissioners decided how much land a miner could have to work their claim with each licence. If they wanted more land they had to pay more licence fees.

Desperate for its revenue, the colonial government decided to grant half the proceeds of fines for licence fees and sly-grogging to individual members of the police force. This, in turn, led to bribery and police corruption as the police were focused on collecting licence fees and fines rather than putting their attention to law enforcement.

Some police were known for their brutality. They had a reputation for treating the miners badly and resorting to thug-like and bullying tactics.

The police on the goldfields have been described as "repressive administrators" [13].

If miners were found to be without a licence, they treated them like criminals.

Rather than combating crime, the police operated as a repressive tax-gathering and surveillance force with digger hunts regularly interrupting the miner's work. Police

---

[13] Mahar, Caitlin "A nation's heritage" https://www.egold.net.au/biogs/EG00008b.htm

demanded to see licences several times a day and forced even those not working to pay[14].

## The military

In those turbulent and chaotic years on the goldfields, the colonial authorities sought the services of the British regiment.

This was the 40th Regiment.

These soldiers were often sent on long tours of duty to some of the furthest outposts of the British Empire. They were sent to the colony of Victoria.

In 1824, the 40th regiment carried out successful punitive expeditions which broke the guerrilla resistance of the Wiradjuri people in the NSW Bathurst region.

With an exploding population, a weak police force, and the difficulty of finding enough police to patrol the goldfields, the military was called in to help.

---

[14] Brown, Richard (2014) "Policing the goldfields" https://richardjohnbr.blogspot.com/2014/01/policing-goldfields.html

This unrest on the goldfields and with it the seeds of rebellion saw the growth of regimental power.

In October 1852, 170 men of the 40th Regiment arrived in Melbourne.

Two years later, members of this Regiment snatched victory by surprise at the Eureka Stockade in Ballarat in 1854.

The 40th regiment remained active in Australia until 1860.

The 12th Regiment, the East Suffolk arrived in 1854 during the time of the Eureka uprising. This regiment also played a leading role in helping to suppress the rebellion.

**Miners' responsibility for law and order**

Because effective law enforcement was lacking on the goldfields, justice was often carried out by the miners themselves.

To control crime, miners might set up their own court and deal out their own punishments. They set up "protection committees" administering their own, and at times brutal justice. Some examples:

- a miner caught stealing was branded with a hot chisel;
- there were reports that some bushrangers were captured and even hanged[15].

The goldfields were dangerous places and with the lack of policing of actual crime, law and order were seriously defective.

---

[15] Sovereign Hill "Law and Order on the Goldfields" https://sovereignhill.com.au/uploads/resources/SovHill-lawandorder-notes-ss1.pdf

"From the time Captain Cook made landfall on Australia's east coast, violent conflict on the Australian frontier started. From this time on, Australia experienced constant warfare on its frontier."

*Marji Hill*

# Chapter 3 – Native Police

First Nations people played a significant role on the goldfields. Those that were recruited into the Native Police Corps became the first enforcers of the law on the goldfields.

First Nations people were "at the epicentre of the Victorian gold epoch" [16].

Not only were they the first police on the goldfields at Ballarat, but First Nations people also participated in the local gold economy and were actively involved in gold mining activities. Some engaged in entrepreneurial activities like selling food and clothing to the miners or they fossicked for gold themselves.

They were well recognised for their unique tracking abilities and their skill at negotiating and navigating the countryside. At times First

---

[16] Cahir, Fred (2012) *Black Gold: Aboriginal People on the Goldfields of Victoria, 1850-1870.* Canberra, ANU Press, p. 8

Nations people assisted the miners. They might act as guides escorting them along traditional trading pathways, helping them to cross waterways, or assisting those who got lost in the bush.

The takeover of traditional lands in New South Wales (NSW) and Victoria by the British followed by the discovery of gold which attracted newcomers from all over the world was a double whammy. Its consequences for First Nations people and their country were cataclysmic.

From the time Captain Cook made landfall on Australia's east coast in 1770, violent conflict on the Australian frontier started.

From this time on, Australia experienced constant and continuous warfare on its frontier.

These frontier wars continued right up to the early 1900s with the last massacre of the First Nations people being recorded in 1928 in the Northern Territory. Several hundred Warlpiri,

Anmatyere and Kaytetye people were massacred for killing a dingo trapper[17].

> The takeover of traditional lands in New South Wales (NSW) and Victoria by the British followed by the discovery of gold which attracted newcomers from all over the world was a double whammy. Its consequences for First Nations people and their country were cataclysmic.

The seeds of war were sown when it became clear that the British were taking over the

---

[17] University of Newcastle (2022) "New evidence reveals Aboriginal massacres committed on extensive scale" https://www.newcastle.edu.au/newsroom/featured/new-evidence-reveals-aboriginal-massacres-committed-on-extensive-scale

continent and were going to occupy the lands belonging to Australia's First Nations people.

Initially, the First Nations who fought in defence of their country greatly underestimated the power of European firearms. Their experience was bloody when they realised that the musket was more powerful than any spear, boomerang, club or other weapons that they had ever devised.

The colonists wanted land for food crops and grazing. They wanted areas where sheep and cattle could graze and flourish. They moved out from the shores of Port Jackson and opened up the plains in NSW and then into Victoria.

The Western District of Victoria had already been penetrated by the British and the traditional First Nations lands had been overrun by more than 300,000 sheep.

From this time in the 1840s, the Victorian countryside became full of white faces with herds of cattle and sheep from the north. A drought in the Monaro region of NSW after

1841 sent people and livestock flooding across the Murray River into northern Victoria.

This invasion of people was overwhelming. Thousands of people were pouring into Victoria.

In what became the colony of Victoria, Christie[18] said that by the end of 1837 there were over 1000 colonists and by 1841 the numbers had risen to over 20,000. First Nations resistance stood little chance.

Victorian First Nations people had been dispossessed in the name of the British Crown on the basis of *terra nullius*, because the British believed at the time that the continent was a land without people.

First Nations people had no legal title to their lands at all under British law and, of course, the British did not recognise the law of the original inhabitants.

By 1850, First Nations resistance began to flag due to the combination of superior and

---

[18] Christie, M. (1979) *Aborigines in Colonial Victoria 1835-86.* Sydney, Sydney University Press, p.57

deadly weapons and military skill. The death rate of the First Nations people in Victoria was high and they had become victims of mounted troops and the Native Police.

## Native Police units

In the nineteenth century, Native Police units were set up in the colony of NSW. These units continued in various forms throughout the continent. They were usually under the command of at least one British officer.

Colonial governments had a policy of recruiting First Nations people into their police forces and was a tactic that was used throughout the Empire for handling Indigenous resistance. It was designed to uphold British law and order.

The recruiting method was to select First Nations men who lived in far distant places. The idea was to try to avoid conflict between First Nations groups, so the strategy was to recruit First Nations police from other groups that were a long way away.

> Colonial governments had a policy of recruiting First Nations people into their police forces and was a tactic that was used throughout the Empire for handling Indigenous resistance. It was designed to uphold British law and order.

The government recognised the cost effectiveness of setting up a Native Police corps because it was a way to minimise wages. Not only was it a way of reducing labour costs, it had the potential to protect

First Nations revenge attacks against the colonists.

## Tracking skills

The great advantage of having First Nations troopers was to exploit their ability to track. Their skill was something well beyond the ambit of most Europeans and this together with their intimate knowledge of the bush was indispensable.

Native Police could track those under surveillance, their skills being utilised when operating in conditions that were poorly mapped or when navigating inhospitable countryside. Their ability to survive in the bush was a bonus to the police force.

Native Police could track down bushrangers or criminals hiding in the bush. Some First Nations men possessed extraordinary powers recognised as being almost magical. They would have been "men of high degree" who possessed specialised skills and powers[19] gained from long specialised training and initiation into a body of secret knowledge and lore.

## First Native Police Corps

The first Native Police Corps was established in 1837 in the Port Phillip District (which at the time part of the colony of NSW).

The concept was proposed by Captain Alexander Maconochie and his idea was seen as a way of "civilising" First Nations men[20].

There were several attempts to set up the Native Police Corps in the Port Phillip District and by 1842 it was established under the command of Henry E. Pulteney Dana. This was a position he held until his death in 1852.

You may wonder why First Nations men would have joined the Native Police. They

---

[19] Elkin, Peter (1977) *Aboriginal Men of High Degree.* 2nd ed. St Lucia, Qld, University of Queensland Press, p.37
[20] Aboriginal History of Yarra
https://aboriginalhistoryofyarra.com.au/8-native-police/

probably joined for pragmatic reasons and their need to survive in catastrophic circumstances.

By doing so they could form alliances with the colonists, as well as to obtain rations to help support their families.

The Native Police became a powerful force and it was a successful strategy for defeating the First Nations guerrilla resistance in the region. The force was feared by other First Nations people.

## Goldfields

As gold finds became commonplace Native Police were used to guard new sites, patrol new goldfields, and to provide law and order. Prior to the gold rush at Ballarat, the Native Police representing government authority were sent to Daisy Hill. They had to guard a site where gold had been discovered on crown land to prevent any unauthorised occupation of the site.

Lieutenant-Governor La Trobe relied on his black mounted police force to enforce the law on the goldfields. His Native Police were sent to patrol and support the gold commissioners on the goldfields and to inspect the mining licences.

It was the role of the Native Police in Victoria that saw the impact of First Nations people on the goldfields.

Members of the Native Police Corps were not local Wadawurrung men; they had been recruited from other parts of Victoria, mainly from around Melbourne[21].

The Native Police arrived in Ballarat in 1851 under the command of Captain Dana, just after the discovery of gold.

They accompanied the officers on their rounds and effectively took action when needed to maintain law and order.

---

[21] Sovereign Hill "The Native Police" https://sovereignhillhiddenhistories.com.au/gold-commissioners-camp/

When in September 1851 Gold Commissioner F. C. Doveton announced that the government was going to introduce gold mining licence fees the announcement inflamed the miners.

The Native Police had a challenging time of it as they had to enforce this unpopular decision.

The presence of the Native Police on the goldfields was met with hostility and anger. Dana and his troopers had the reputation for using dictatorial tactics to control law and order.

This led to unrest. Their use of "heavy-handed tactics" was greatly feared by those they policed.

Native Policeman

It got to a stage where Dana had to request reinforcements to help control the festering anger and hostility of the miners.

The Native Police were a potent, imposing and fearsome force. Physically they looked splendid in their uniforms on their horses.

They were ever ready to support the authority of the gold commissioners checking on the claims and making sure that licences were paid.

**Duties of the Native Police**

Their duties were numerous. They had to

- assist the Gold Commissioners
- patrol the bush
- control frontier violence
- track people lost in the bush
- check for prisoners
- patrol new gold finds
- act as guards at the Pentridge prison

- carry messages and mail to colonial outposts
- provide protection for the Gold Escort

Even members of the Native Police Corps got caught by gold fever. Members of the Native Police Corps would fossick for gold as did many other First Nations people[22].

Many a time Native Police had to go against their own people[23]. They had to implement the orders of their commander because they feared punishment if they didn't comply.

Before he died in 1852 Captain Dana had trouble keeping his troopers together; they kept deserting. Some turned to alcohol. Others felt compelled to enact the orders of Captain Dana as they were threatened with imprisonment and harm if they failed to carry out his orders.

---

[22] Cahir, Fred (2012) *Black Gold: Aboriginal People on the Goldfields of Victoria, 1850-1870.* Canberra, ANU Press, p.23

[23] https://www.deadlystory.com/page/culture/history/Native_Police_Corps_established)

Some Native Police left the Corps and returned to their families; others went to work on pastoral properties, and there were those who decided to search for gold themselves and used it for trade.

It was difficult to recruit new members.

After their Commander Dana died in 1852, the Native Police contingent was disbanded.

Following this time, a contingent of heavily armed police was introduced.

## Queensland force

From 1848 another Native Police force was organised in NSW. This mostly operated within the borders of the later colony of Queensland. The NSW Legislative Council had passed an Act allowing sufficient money to establish another small corps of Native Police[24].

---

[24] National Museum of Australia "NSW Native Police" https://www.nma.gov.au/defining-moments/resources/nsw-native-police

"The violence which had started with the Native Police in the southern colonies had migrated north."

*Marji Hill*

# Chapter 4 – The Queensland Frontier

In August 1848, just before the official discovery of gold in New South Wales (NSW), Frederick Walker was appointed to command the Native Police.

Walker recruited fourteen troopers. He made his selection from four different groups of First Nations people in the Murrumbidgee, Murray and Edwards river areas of southern NSW.

Walker formed and trained his recruits into a cohesive group. Some months later they operated on the Queensland frontier. Their purpose was to suppress First Nations resistance making way for colonisation.

Being far from the colonial authority's heartland, Walker implemented tactics that involved revenge and reprisal.

Attacks on First Nations people were chilling. These were retaliative ambushes and punitive actions against them.

Walker and his troopers were successful. Armed with superior weapons and ammunition they pursued their First Nations opponents in Queensland's tough and dangerous country.

Walker expanded his force. His tactics were violent. It is said that at times he was simply intent on annihilating groups of First Nations people[25].

Eventually, as a result of his violent and brutal methods there was a government inquiry in 1854 and Walker was sacked.

The violence which had started with the Native Police in the southern colonies had migrated to the northern frontier.

---

[25] National Museum of Australia. https://www.nma.gov.au/defining-moments/resources/nsw-native-police

Punitive expedition

## Systematic killing

From 1859 on, when Queensland became a colony, the pastoral frontier expanded vigorously to the west and the north in Queensland.

The opening up of the frontier was characterised by constant warfare and conflict between the European colonists and First Nations people.

Raymond Evans[26] argues that in Queensland the policy of the settlers was to wreak the most terrible revenge possible on First Nations people.

Native Police were used to systematically kill First Nations people which was euphemistically called "dispersing".

They were a symbol of white colonial attitudes toward First Nations people and their activities were part of a "widespread campaign of frontier violence"[27].

In Queensland, New South Wales and Victoria colonial authorities as they did in other parts of the British Empire used armed Indigenous forces for colonisation purposes.

Their role was to protect the land owners, the gold miners and settlers on the frontier.

---

[26] Evans, R., Saunders, K. & Cronin, K. (1988) Race Relations in Colonial Queensland. St.Lucia, University of Queensland Press, p.50

[27] Richards, Jonathan (2009) "Native Police" https://www.qhatlas.com.au/content/native-police

The Native Police efforts at "protection" in reality meant patrols to kill First Nations people who were in turn trying to protect their land, and their families. There were literally hundreds of such episodes.

The British would probably not have succeeded in fully colonising Queensland in just a few decades as they did, without First Nations assistance of the Native Police force.

Any First Nations resistance to British expansion of the Queensland frontier was ruthlessly crushed by Native Police led by British officers.

## Recruiting

Colonial authorities had difficulties recruiting skilled Europeans into their police forces so an option was to recruit First Nations men who were more effective in Queensland's difficult terrain. They could function well in places that were inhospitable to Europeans.

The Victorian colonial authorities, likewise, had understood the value of having First

Nations recruits in their police force. In particular, they appreciated their tracking skills.

Wages for the Native Police were fear and death and a few pennies a day[28].

When First Nations people were recruited to the Native Police colonial authorities were fully aware that there was significant enmity between First Nations groups. They capitalised on this.

Troopers would be recruited from far distant places where it was unlikely that they had any close kinship ties with the people who were to be their most likely victims.

Traditional enmities were exploited and they implemented tactics of divide and rule.

Native Police were also recruited from places where First Nations people camped and were experiencing hunger, disease and malnutrition like fringe camps on the outskirts of towns.

---

[28] Richards, Jonathan (2009) *ibid.*

Native Police recruits wearing military caps had dark blue jackets and striped trousers.

Desertion was a major challenge.

When First Nations men realised what they had to do many ran away from the force soon after joining. Richards[29] says some may have left after they were treated badly by the British officers like being beaten or whipped. Others were shot.

## Gold

As colonisation expanded to the northern frontiers the new settlers had their sights set on Queensland's resources with its vast expanses of land, gold, minerals, and timber.

From 1867 on through the 1870s and 1880s, gold was discovered in central and northern Queensland.

The discovery of gold transformed Queensland's history and landscape attracting

---

[29] Richards, Jonathan (2009) *ibid.*

people from other colonies and countries in different parts of the world.

The digger with shovel and prospecting dish was in the van of the spread of settlement north[30]. Just like it was in the southern colonies, the impact on the First Nations people of the Queensland discoveries of gold was equally devastating.

Gold was found on a cattle property at Ravenswood in 1868. A year later there was a township with over 700 people.

With the gold finds, hundreds of heavily armed men dug for gold in every gully and in every creek bed.

The battle for Country was fought fiercely and bravely by the First Nations people against the miners.

These wars for Country were just as fiercely fought in central and western Australia as they were in the east.

---

[30] Pike, (1996) *Queensland Frontiers*. Brisbane, Glenville Pike. p.215

In the newly occupied pastoral districts of Queensland, the Native Police were the instrument of colonial policy bringing with it a reign of terror and violence.

Members of the Native Police were involved in the brutal deaths of a large number of First Nations people in Queensland[31]. They were always on patrol watching out for resistance. Those that were thought to be responsible were tracked down and killed.

At night time troopers would surround a First Nations camp and then at dawn they would attack. Sometimes the bodies were burnt to cover up the massacres[32].

Richards[33] identifies five deadly attacks on First Nations people by Native Police who would take revenge on those who attacked invading colonists.

---

[31] Richards, Jonathan (2009) "Native Police" https://www.qhatlas.com.au/content/native-police
[32] Richards, Jonathan *ibid.*
[33] Richards, Jonathan (2008) *The Secret War: a True History of Queensland's Native Police.* St Lucia, Qld, University of Queensland Press, 2008, p.30-35.

The killing of First Nations people was commonplace in Queensland and the purpose was one thing only - to exterminate.

These actions brought about by British policy in the colonies were considered a "normal" part of most colonisation schemes for hundreds of years.

**Making sense of the past**

The expansion of the Queensland frontier was brutal, to say the least.

The disturbing thing about Queensland's Native Police was that most of the men responsible for these violent massacres were First Nations people themselves while acting under the orders of their British officers[34]. These white officers had small detachments of just six or seven troopers.

---

[34] Moodie, Georgia (2019) "Coming to terms with the brutal history of Queensland's Native Mounted Police" https://www.abc.net.au/news/2019-07-24/native-mounted-police-indigenous-history-aboriginal-troopers/11296384

Moodie[35] refers to the research of Lynley Wallis who says that the whole purpose of the Native Police in Queensland was to move First Nations people off their lands to make way for colonisation.

The Queensland Native Police had to protect the pastoralists, miners and colonialists on the frontier. They had to achieve this by whatever means were necessary.

Their method of "protection" was to mount patrols and to kill. The victims were First Nations people who were trying to protect their land, lives and loved ones[36].

Descendants of the Queensland Native Police today try to make sense of this past. It's a

---

[35] Moodie, Georgia (2019) "Coming to terms with the brutal history of Queensland's Native Mounted Police" https://www.abc.net.au/news/2019-07-24/native-mounted-police-indigenous-history-aboriginal-troopers/11296384

[36] Wallis, Lynley, Barker, Bryce & Burke, Heather (2018) "How unearthing Queensland's 'native police 'camps gives us a window onto colonial violence" https://theconversation.com/how-unearthing-queenslands-native-police-camps-gives-us-a-window-onto-colonial-violence-100814

legacy that for many is complicated, difficult and hard to understand.

Truth-telling, however, is necessary for understanding the past and paving the way for the healing process to begin.

"With thousands flooding the goldfields,
and gold being plentiful,
temptation was there to steal gold.
Newspapers were full of reports
of bushranger exploits."

*Marji Hill*

# Chapter 5 – Bushrangers

Bushrangers are part of the Australian story and with the gold discoveries great wealth for many was created. Given the lure of so much wealth, bushranging gained momentum, particularly between the years 1851 and 1880.

Bushrangers might have been villains but some became heroes in Australia's legendary past.

Gold was an attraction for bushrangers who were either petty thieves or cold-blooded bandits.

Miners had a choice of keeping and hiding their gold or sending it in Gold Escorts to the cities for safekeeping. Either way, there was a risk as gold was such a target for bushrangers.

Convicts were sent to Australian penal settlements where they had to endure long hours of hard labour. Life was tough, food was in short supply. Life was cruel.

Many absconded. These were desperate men, escapees who would live and hide in the bush. They lived a life of crime and stole to survive rather than endure their existence as prisoners.

There were others who were not escaped convicts. Bushrangers became symbols of rebellion against colonial authorities. They were celebrated for their bravery, rough chivalry and colourful personalities. They were wild young men wanting to get rich quick or to make their fame as a result of their notorious exploits[37].

Bushrangers were usually expert horsemen; they could navigate the bush and they could easily outrun the law.

While the villainy of bushrangers is sometimes forgotten their memories have

---

[37] NSW Department of Primary Industries (2000) "Life on the goldfields: bushrangers – the lure of gold"
http://www.dpi.nsw.gov.au/__data/assets/pdf_file/0006/109941/life-on-the-goldfields-bushrangers-the-lure-of-gold.pdf

more to do with the romance of their daring adventures, their amazing horsemanship, their ability to survive and hide in the bush, and their challenge to colonial authorities.

> While the villainy of bushrangers is sometimes forgotten their memories have more to do with the romance of their daring adventures, their amazing horsemanship, their ability to survive and hide in the bush, and their challenge to colonial authorities.

## Early bushrangers

Bushranging started in the early days of the colony.

One of the early bushrangers was a First Nations resistance fighter named Musquito (c.1780 – 1825). From the Hawkesbury River and Broken Bay regions of New South Wales

(NSW) Musquito fought against colonial expansion on Australia's east coast[38].

In 1805 Musquito was captured. He was transported to Norfolk Island most likely for leading attacks against the British settlers who were invading his country along the lower Hawkesbury River. Norfolk Island was a penal settlement at the time of Musquito, located approximately 1,000 kilometres off the east coast of Australia.

Musquito was possibly a Kuring-gai man from around Broken Bay in NSW although Parry[39] suggests he was an Eora man, born on the north shore of Port Jackson, NSW.

Musquito led many of the raids on settlers and their property along the NSW Central coast.

From Norfolk Island in 1813, Musquito was sent to Launceston in Tasmania, then called Van Dieman's Land.

---

[38] Hill, Marji (2021) *Australian Aboriginal History: 5 Stories of Indigenous Heroes*. Gold Coast, Qld, The Prison Tree Press.
[39] Parry, Naomi (2006) https://adb.anu.edu.au/biography/musquito-13124

The Lieutenant-Governor at the time, Colonel William Sorell, sought Musquito's help in tracking down bushranger, Michael Howe. Sorrell had been impressed with Musquito's abilities as a tracker, so in return for doing this Musquito was promised his freedom to return to his people in NSW.

In 1818 Musquito was put to work as a stockman for one of the British settlers, Edward Lord. In October of that year, Musquito succeeded in helping to find the bushranger, Michael Howe, and kill him. However, Sorrell broke his promise of freedom.

In about 1819 Musquito, very antagonistic towards the white settlers, became a bushranger himself. He went into the Tasmanian bush and joined the Laremairremener people from Oyster Bay.

They joined forces and ran guerrilla campaigns against the British.

Musquito's expertise as a guerrilla resistance fighter, together with his knowledge of the English language and English customs, were assets to the local Laremairremener people who wanted to retaliate against the English aggression.

Uniting with "Black Jack", another resistance fighter, Musquito led a series of successful attacks on outlying farms on the east coast of Tasmania in 1823 and in 1824. He is alleged to have participated in offensives which resulted in the death of several colonists.

The military was then on his trail.

**Capture**

Lieutenant-Governor George Arthur offered a reward for Musquito's capture and he was captured in 1825.

Musquito's several years of successful guerrilla warfare and bushranging came to an end when two bushrangers-cum-bounty hunters led by a renegade called Teague tracked him down.

A wounded Musquito and his fellow resistance fighter, Black Jack, were taken back to Hobart where they were eventually publicly hanged on 24 February 1825.

## Mary Cockerill, female bushranger

There was a female bushranger in that same era, and again in Van Dieman's Land, a First Nations woman by the name of Mary Cockerill[40].

Mary Cockerill (c1798-1819) was also known as Black Mary.

She lived and worked with the Cockerill family. Described as "articulate, brave, and resolute"[41] she wore clothes derived from both European and Indigenous styles: skins, calico and feathers.

As a teenager, Mary met the English bushranger, Michael Howe (1787-1818)[42]. He was a convict who had been transported for seven years for his activities as a

---

[40] Terra Australis Readers & Writers Festival https://www.terroraustralisfestival.com/mary-cockerill 2021
[41] Von Stieglitz, K. R. (2006) "Howe, Michael (1787–1818)" https://adb.anu.edu.au/biography/howe-michael-2206
[42] SBS https://www.sbs.com.au/gold/lawless-and-disorderly/

highwayman. Howe arrived in Van Dieman's Land in 1812 and was assigned to service with the merchant, John Ingle.

Both Mary Cockerill and Michael Howe had been with English families. In 1815 they escaped, fled and joined the Whitehead Gang.

In her career as a bushranger Mary Cockerill utilised her Indigenous skills. Given her amazing knowledge of the bush she would assist in helping the gang navigate that unforgiving terrain.

With her help the gang managed to evade capture.

In 1817 a contingent of the 46th Regiment pursued them and both Mary Cockerill and Michael Howe were both found some 75 kilometres away from Hobart.

Michael Howe eventually betrayed Mary.

She was unable to keep up with him and he shot her. While he attempted to kill her and while she did have serious injuries, Mary did recover.

An outraged Mary joined the regiment helping it in the hunt for Michael Howe.

The Lieutenant-Governor at the time was the same Colonel William Sorell who sought Musquito's help in tracking down Michael Howe.

Michael Howe was eventually caught in 1818, was killed by Musquito and decapitated.

Mary got a pardon and went to Sydney and started a new life there. After contracting a lung disease, she returned to Hobart where she died in 1819.

**Bushrangers of the gold rush**

Bushrangers of the gold rush days usually became thieves by choice. After all, gold was a huge attraction.

While every effort was made to protect the gold there was every possibility that a Gold Escort could be held up and robbed by bushrangers.

There were no banks on the goldfields[43] so miners with their gold were easy targets for bushrangers as were travellers journeying on isolated and lonely roads.

Gold miners, if they had to travel between the goldfields and the city had to travel in groups for protection. It was too dangerous to travel alone. It was particularly dangerous when gold was being carried.

Bushrangers usually operated in rural areas because the bush was their place to hide and escape after committing a crime. They stole horses, gold, personal possessions, money, mail, saddles, guns, ammunition, clothes and food.

Most had an excellent knowledge of the countryside and they were highly skilled with horses and guns.

Bushrangers took advantage of people living in isolated homesteads, where they would

---

[43] Webber, Kimberley (2001) *Law and Order on the Goldfields.* South Yarra, Vic, Macmillan. p. 13

force them to cook food or to provide shelter - sometimes at gun point.

## Australia's largest gold robbery

Bushrangers in the time of the gold rushes were a new generation of outlaws. Among some of them were Frank Gardiner, Ben Hall, Captain Moonlite and Ned Kelly.

In 1862 eight bushrangers plotted Australia's largest gold robbery over a bottle of liquor in a small house near Forbes in country NSW[44]. The plan was to hold up a Gold Escort which was transporting gold from Forbes to Orange and then onto Sydney.

The leader of the bushranger gang was Frank Gardiner. Another member of the gang was Ben Hall who went on to become one of Australia's notorious bushrangers.

---

[44] Fisher, Alexandra (2018) "Gin, guns and getaways: How a bushranger gang pulled off Australia's largest gold heist" https://www.abc.net.au/news/2018-08-26/how-a-bushranger-gang-pulled-off-australias-biggest-gold-heist/10152580

Ned Kelly's armour

The gang ambushed the Escort and got off with the haul of gold that would have been worth a staggering $10 million today.

Given the amount of gold they stole, together with the fact that they killed two officers, they became the most wanted men not only in NSW but in the British Empire.

### Heroes in folk law

With thousands flooding the goldfields, and gold being plentiful temptation was there to steal gold. Newspapers were full of reports of bushranger exploits.

They became feared throughout the colony and while they might have lived a life of crime, some have become enshrined in Australia's history and culture.

"Sam Poo is recognised as Australia's first Chinese bushranger."

*Erin Wen Ai Chew*

# Chapter 6 – Sam Poo

Sam Poo (c1835-1865) was a Chinese bushranger who was active in New South Wales (NSW). It is unusual to hear of a Chinese bushranger but Sam Poo is recognised[45] as an Australian first.

The name "Sam Poo" was not his original, Chinese name and was probably given to him by the police and the public at the time. His real name was possibly Li Hang Chiak.

Sam Poo came to Australia from Singapore in the 1860s.

He was heard of in NSW at the Talbragar goldfield which was situated between Dunedoo and Mudgee. There were plenty of

---

[45] Chew, Erin Wen Ai (2021) "Meet Sam Poo' – Australia's first and only Singaporean Chinese Bushranger" https://beingasianaustralian.net/2021/09/03/meet-sam-poo-australias-first-and-only-singaporean-chinese-bushranger/

miners who were not successful at finding gold and Sam Poo was one of them.

*Sam Poo*

He set up his camp on the outskirts of the goldfield.

Sam Poo was an unfriendly sort of character who was not very well liked either by the

Chinese or by the Europeans. He was surly and he got the nickname, Cranky Sam.

## Life of crime

Sam Poo started his life of crime when he stole gold from his countrymen, fellow Chinese miners.

In early January 1865 according to the Hill End Family History[46], Sam Poo disappeared from the diggings and then within a few days at an isolated spot along the Mudgee Road he bailed up ten Chinese prospectors at pistol point.

The Chinese had concealed gold dust in a calico pouch under their pigtails. Sam Poo stole the gold.

Sam Poo, with a sawn-off rifle and pistol, held up travellers who journeyed on foot on the Gulgong-Mudgee Road. He did this for several weeks.

_____

[46] Hill End Family History "Sam Poo"
https://hillendfamilyhistory.com/history/bushrangers/sam-poo/

At the end of January 1865, Poo was seen on *Billabong Station* a property near Dubbo. The story goes was that he was having some interaction with the daughter of Elizabeth and Robert Golding. Poo ran off when Robert Golding came to his daughter's assistance.

Apparently, Poo had been hiding on the property and had lived off flour which was in one of the sheds.

The Hill End Family History[47] version of the story of Sam Poo, is that he attacked and raped a woman on 8 February 1865. It is said that he held the woman prisoner but let her go in the evening; he then disappeared into the night.

In that same month, Sam Poo killed the police constable John Ward who had been trying to capture the bushranger on his own. Ward was the officer-in-charge of Coonabarabran police station.

When Sam Poo saw the policeman he ran into the bush. Ward gave chase and ordered Poo

---

[47] Hill End Family History "Sam Poo"*Ibid.*

to drop his weapon. There was a shootout; Ward was wounded, and Sam Poo disappeared.

The mortally wounded policeman was found by a squatter, James Francis Plunkett, the owner of *Birriwa Station* where the shootout took place.

Plunkett took Ward to his homestead and sent for a doctor. By the time the doctor eventually arrived, Ward was way beyond medical help.

After the murder of Ward, police troopers organised a large-scale manhunt. For two weeks an armed and mounted posse searched the district for him but Poo couldn't be found.

Eventually a black tracker, Henry (Harry) Hughes, joined the manhunt. In mid-February 1865 Hughes and mounted police located Poo in an area of scrub.

There was a fight. Sam Poo was overpowered and seriously wounded ending up with a fractured skull.

After lengthy medical treatment and recuperation, Sam Poo was transported to

Bathurst to stand trial for the murder of John Ward and the attempted murder of Henry Hughes[48].

Poo at the age of 35 was sentenced to death. He was hung at Bathurst Gaol on 19 December 1865.

The execution was watched by three Chinese prisoners and a dozen civilians.

There are different versions of his execution. One says he was unconscious of his fate and was executed without speaking a word.

In another version of the story, Sam Poo's last words was a request that he did not wish to see any of his countrymen.

---

[48] Crosby, Heather (2015) "Australia's only Chinese bushranger remembered 150 years on"
https://www.dailyliberal.com.au/story/2866513/australias-only-chinese-bushranger-remembered-150-years-on/

"Mary Ann Bugg was a proud Worimi woman, a mother of an estimated fifteen children, and one of Australia's early female bushrangers."

*Marji Hill*

# Chapter 7 – Mary Ann Bugg

In Australia's legendary past bushrangers were bandits who bailed up travellers, and stole their money, gold, and possessions. But many were celebrated in history for their bravery, chivalry, and the way they outran and ridiculed colonial authorities.

While most bushrangers were men, some of them were women:

- Mary Cockerill (c.1798-1819) was a First Nations woman who operated in Van Dieman's Land

- Mary Ann Bugg (1934-1905) was a First Nations woman

- Jessie Hickman (1890-1936) born Elizabeth Jessie Hunt was another First Nations female bushranger. She was known as the Lady Bushranger.

Mary Ann Bugg was a Worimi woman. Her husband was Frederick Wordsworth Ward (1835 - 1870) better known as the bushranger hero, Captain Thunderbolt.

Mary Ann Bugg

## Worimi people

Worimi people are the traditional custodians of a large area of land that is bounded by the four rivers - the Hunter, the Manning, the Allyn and the Patterson Rivers.

The Worimi, as with other First Nations people, have a complex system of family relationships. In Worimi kinship every person knows their kin and their country.

This extended network of family relationships is central to the way culture is passed on and how society is organised.

Kinship systems define where a person fits into the community, binding people together in relationships of sharing, obligation and responsibility.

Frederick Wordsworth Ward (1835-1870), better known as Captain Thunderbolt, was married to Mary Ann Bugg. This meant he was part of that system of kinship involving reciprocal relationships that developed between Indigenous and Europeans.

Captain Thunderbolt got notoriety for escaping from Cockatoo Island, the island prison on Sydney Harbour, and being the longest-roaming bushranger in Australian history.

Mary Ann Bugg lived in the era when the New South Wales (NSW) government was recruiting black trackers and Native Police to remove First Nations people from their country so as to open the way for colonial expansion.

What has been described as "organised squadrons"[49], these members of the Native Police had no kinship connections or sympathy for local clans.

**Expert bush woman**

Mary Ann Bugg was an expert horsewoman and she could successfully navigate dense bushland. Mary was Fred Ward's right-hand

---

[49] Dulaney, Michael (2019) "Mary Ann Bugg, the Aboriginal bushranger erased from Australian folklore" https://www.abc.net.au/news/2019-11-17/mary-ann-bugg-bushranger-partner-captain-thunderbolt/11699992

person and chief lieutenant as he roamed the New England region of NSW.

She assisted him as he held up travellers, and robbed inns, and coaches all the while eluding the police. Mary Ann was his scout, informer, lover and confidante and she bore him several children.

When Fred Ward died from a gunshot wound on 25 May 1870, he left behind an enduring mystery. Legend has it that he had £20,000 in gold and notes that he stole during his time bushranging.

## Upbringing

Mary Ann was born at Stroud, a small country town one hour north of Newcastle and near Gloucester in NSW.

Her mother was a First Nations woman. Her father had been a convict who had been transported for life on the charge of stealing meat. In 1834 he was granted a Ticket of Leave.

His name was James Brigg but he changed his name to Bugg.

Mary had a younger brother but her story varies as there are many and varied accounts about Mary Ann Bugg.

According to Hill End Family History[50], both Mary Ann and her brother were sent to a boarding school in Sydney by the Australian Agricultural Company. Stroud was the headquarters for this publicly funded company.

In this era of history for First Nations children, it was uncommon to get an education. But as a result of Mary Ann's schooling, she learned to read and write which was to prove invaluable during her bushranging career.

When she was eleven years of age she returned to Stroud and worked as a domestic.

---

[50] Hill End Family History
https://hillendfamilyhistory.com/history/bushrangers/mary-ann-bugg/

At the young age of fourteen she married Edmund Baker who got work on a property near Mudgee which was owned by the Garbutt family near Mudgee. Mrs Sarah Ann Garbutt was Fred Ward's sister.

In 1856 Fred Ward and his nephew, John Garbutt, were sent to prison for ten years at Cockatoo Island for receiving stolen horses.

They served just four years and were released on Ticket of Leave. By this time Mary Ann had either separated from her husband or else he had died.

Fred Ward followed Mary Ann to Stroud. By late 1860 Fred and Mary Ann were married in the Anglican church at Stroud.

Every month, Fred Ward would go back to Mudgee for a muster and for the trip he would borrow a horse from his employer.

In October 1861 he was arrested for arriving late for the muster and for being in possession of a horse for which he could not prove ownership.

## Cockatoo Island

Ward was sent back to Cockatoo Island to serve the rest of his sentence plus he got another three years for horse stealing. Two weeks later Mary Ann gave birth to their first child, Marina Emily Ward.

Legend has it that Mary Ann put her baby into care. She then apparently moved to Balmain in Sydney to be close to Cockatoo Island. She got a job there as a housemaid using the name Louisa Mason.

Mary Ann would visit her husband on Cockatoo Island taking him food. She also brought him a file so that he could cut through the chains.

The gaolers encouraged the presence of sharks around Cockatoo Island by putting offal into the water. In September 1863, Fred Ward and his mate Fred Britten made their escape by diving into the dangerous waters and swimming to Balmain.

Mary Ann may have helped with the escape. The Hill End version of the story[51] is that she got them to hide in a disused boiler in the industrial area of Balmain while they waited for the police to stop their search.

The escapees then moved north followed by Mary Ann some weeks later.

## Bushranging life

Once back in the Hunter region, Fred Ward held up the Rutherford tollbar. This was the beginning of Fred Ward's bushranging days and he became known as Captain Thunderbolt.

From 1863 to 1867, Frederick Ward (Captain Thunderbolt) and Mary Ann lived as bushrangers. This ultimately culminated in Ward being shot to death in Uralla in 1870 by which time she had born him several children.

---

[51] Hill End Family History *Ibid.*

For six and a half years Thunderbolt was part of a bushranging gang which operated from south Queensland to the Hunter Valley, from Stroud to Bourke and Mudgee, and for a time around Armidale and Uralla.

Mary might have been part of the gang and during the time had four children. She certainly assisted Thunderbolt with food and shelter in the mountainous areas[52].

She taught Thunderbolt to read and helped him to outwit the police[53].

Mary Ann was clever. She could go into a township incognito and get supplies. She also collected information about police and coach movements and was attuned to local gossip.

Mary Ann had an extraordinary hearing and many a time she saved Captain Thunderbolt. She would place her ear to the ground to receive warning of approaching horses.

---

[52] SBS  https://www.sbs.com.au/gold/lawless-and-disorderly/
[53] SBS https://www.sbs.com.au/gold/lawless-and-disorderly/

Heffernan[54] refers to reports that in 1865, while police were hunting for Ward they came across a very pregnant Mary Ann in Thunderbolt's camp. Heffernan says the *Maitland Mercury* reported how she "sprung up like a tigress" and taunted the police because they should have been apprehending Thunderbolt and not her.

When she was arrested, the police were obliged to leave Mary Ann at a nearby property while they continued to hunt for the male bushrangers. Miraculously, upon the police's departure her contractions appear to have ceased and when Thunderbolt came by the station, Mary Ann and the children escaped.

Mary wore the clothes of a young man wearing knee-length Wellington boots, moleskin trousers, a Crimean shirt, a monkey jacket and a cabbage tree hat.

In 1867 Mary Ann was arrested for the third and final time. Her arrest was for stealing

---

[54] Heffernan, Elizabeth "Mary Ann Bugg (1834-1905)" https://www.rahs.org.au/mary-ann-bugg-1834-1905/

twelve yards of fabric and she was sentenced to three months in jail.

She wrote to Governor Sir John Young and explained that her imprisonment was unlawful and this together with public support in her favour, she was released.

## Death?

One retelling of Mary Ann's story in the Hill End[55] version is that she died a tragic death from pneumonia in 1867 and was mourned by Thunderbolt. A grieving Fred Ward is said to have asked a Mrs Bradford to care for the dying Mary Ann. Mrs Bradford found Mary Ann in a bush shelter close by and took her home and she died overnight.

Not long after her death, the press reported that Louisa Mason, alias Yellow Long, had died of pneumonia.

---

[55] Hill End Family History
https://hillendfamilyhistory.com/history/bushrangers/mary-ann-bugg/

The identity of this woman remains uncertain. It could have been Mary Ann Bugg. She had used the name Louisa Mason when she was in Balmain.

Hefferman[56] says that there is another version of Mary Bugg's story. The woman that died was not Mary Ann. It was very likely to have been Louisa Mason, a First Nations woman who rode with Thunderbolt and had become his lover.

Dulaney[57] refers to Carol Baxter's research that Mary Ann survived long after the death of her husband, Captain Thunderbolt, and that they had parted ways in 1867.

Mary Ann had left Thunderbolt. It was another First Nation woman, Louisa Mason, according to Foster[58] that had died. Foster says that after Mary Ann became pregnant

---

[56] Heffernan, Elizabeth "Mary Ann Bugg (1834-1905)" op cit

[57] Dulaney, Michael (2019) "Mary Ann Bugg, the Aboriginal bushranger erased from Australian folklore" https://www.abc.net.au/news/2019-11-17/mary-ann-bugg-bushranger-partner-captain-thunderbolt/11699992

[58] Foster, Meg "Bugg, Mary Ann (1834-1905)" https://peopleaustralia.anu.edu.au/biography/bugg-mary-ann-29654

with her last child to Ward, the couple parted ways for good.

Thunderbolt died at Uralla in 1870, but Mary Ann went on to outlive the famous bushranger.

After giving birth to at least five more children, becoming a nurse, purchasing land and marrying her longest-term partner, John Burrows, she died at the age of seventy in Mudgee on 22 April 1905.

In Baxter's history, Mary Ann died there the mother of several children.

As Thunderbolt's lieutenant and herself an inventive and resourceful bushranger, Mary Ann's entire life past her bushranging days exemplifies her courage as a partner, mother, and First Nations woman.

Mary Ann Bugg was a proud Worimi woman, a mother of an estimated fifteen children, and one of Australia's early female bushrangers.

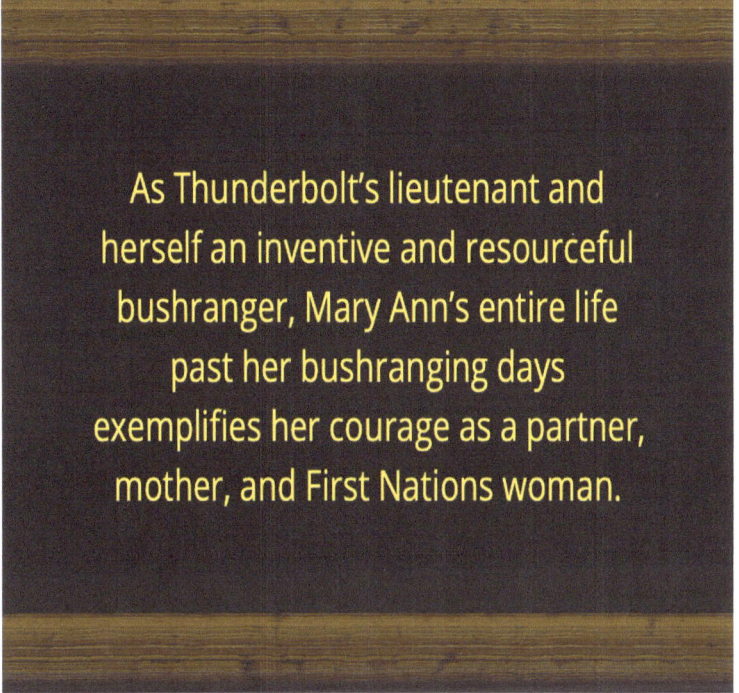

## In summary

After gold was discovered in 1851 its magnetic attraction meant thousands of gold-seekers and wealth came to the Australian bush. In those early unregulated and chaotic days there was a need for law and order on the goldfields. As desperate miners descended onto the diggings there was a huge increase in crime.

Not only was there lawlessness but for travellers on roads between the diggings and the cities, armed robberies and violence were common. There was a drastic shortage of police at the time because in July 1851, all but two of Melbourne's forty police had resigned and taken off to the goldfields.

There was considerable fear for public order. There was not much of it and this lack of attention to crime on the part of the colonial administration led to increased calls for law enforcement and police protection. With the lack of policing of actual crime, law and order on the goldfields was seriously defective.

The colonial authorities needed help in establishing law and order and for this they got the assistance of paramilitary police and the military.

Lieutenant-Governor La Trobe relied on his black mounted police force to enforce the law on the goldfields. His Native Police, the first law enforcers on the goldfields, were sent to patrol and support the gold commissioners and to inspect the mining licences.

To counter First Nations resistance prior to the discovery of gold, colonial governments had a policy of recruiting First Nations people into a police force. This was a tactic that was used throughout the Empire. It was a way of dealing with Indigenous resistance and was designed to uphold British law and order.

The Native Police, looking splendid in their uniforms, were a potent, imposing and fearsome force. Their presence on the goldfields was met with hostility and anger because they got a reputation for using dictatorial and heavy-handed tactics to control law which was greatly feared by those they policed.

As the Australian frontier expanded north and Queensland became a colony, its opening up was characterised by constant warfare and conflict between the European colonists and First Nations people.

The policy of the British settlers at the time was to wreak the most terrible revenge possible on the First Nations people. Native Police were used to systematically kill First

Nations people, their activities being part of a campaign of frontier violence to advance colonisation.

The British would probably not have succeeded in fully colonising Queensland in just a few decades as they did, without the assistance of the Native Police force.

The lure of gold was very much part of the expanding frontier and gold itself became a target for theft. With thousands migrating to the goldfields, and gold being plentiful, the temptation was there to steal gold.

Newspapers were full of stories of bushranger exploits.

Bushranging gained momentum and the bushranger became part of the Australian story. In history, often their villainy was forgotten.

Bushrangers were remembered for their daring exploits, their ability to negotiate the bush, their horsemanship and their challenge to the colonial authorities.

They were feared throughout the colony and while they might have lived a life of crime some were enshrined in Australia's history and culture.

# SOURCES

The author acknowledges the following sources of information:

Australian Broadcasting Commission https://www.abc.net.au/news/2019-07-24/native-mounted-police-indigenous-history-aboriginal-troopers/11296384

Aboriginal History of Yarra https://aboriginalhistoryofyarra.com.au/8-native-police/

Barlow, Alex and Hill, Marji (2000) *The Macmillan Encyclopedia Australia's Aboriginal Peoples.* South Yarra, Vic, Macmillan.

Brown, Richard (2014) "Policing the goldfields" https://richardjohnbr.blogspot.com/2014/01/policing-goldfields.html

Cahir, Fred (2012) *Black Gold: Aboriginal People on the Goldfields of Victoria, 1850-1870.* Canberra, ANU Press.

Chew, Erin Wen Ai (2021) "Meet Sam Poo' – Australia's first and only Singaporean Chinese Bushranger" https://beingasianaustralian.net/2021/09/03/meet-sam-poo-australias-first-and-only-singaporean-chinese-bushranger/

Christie, M. (1979) *Aborigines in Colonial Victoria 1835-86.* Sydney, Sydney University Press.

Crosby, Heather (2015) "Australia's only Chinese bushranger remembered 150 years on" https://www.dailyliberal.com.au/story/2866513/australias-only-chinese-bushranger-remembered-150-years-on/

https://www.deadlystory.com/page/culture/history/Native_Police_Corps_established)

Dulaney, Michael (2019) "Mary Ann Bugg, the Aboriginal bushranger erased from Australian folklore" https://www.abc.net.au/news/2019-11-17/mary-ann-bugg-bushranger-partner-captain-thunderbolt/11699992

Electronic Encyclopedia of Gold in Australia "A nation's heritage" https://www.egold.net.au/biogs/EG00143b.htm

Elkin, Peter (1977) *Aboriginal Men of High Degree.* 2nd ed. St Lucia, Qld, University of Queensland Press

Evans,R., Saunders, K. & Cronin, K. (1988) *Race Relations in Colonial Queensland.* St.Lucia, University of Qld Press.

Fisher, Alexandra (2018) "Gin, guns and getaways: How a bushranger gang pulled off Australia's largest gold heist" https://www.abc.net.au/news/2018-08-26/how-a-bushranger-gang-pulled-off-australias-biggest-gold-heist/10152580

Foster, Meg "Bugg, Mary Ann (1834-1905)" https://peopleaustralia.anu.edu.au/biography/bugg-mary-ann-29654

Grassby, Al and Hill, Marji (1988) *Six Australian Battlefields*. North Ryde, NSW, Angus & Robertson.

Heffernan, Elizabeth "Mary Ann Bugg (1834-1905)" https://www.rahs.org.au/mary-ann-bugg-1834-1905/

Hill End Family History "Sam Poo" https://hillendfamilyhistory.com/history/bushrangers/sam-poo/

Hill End Family History "Mary Ann Bugg" https://hillendfamilyhistory.com/history/bushrangers/mary-ann-bugg/

Hill, Marji (2021) *Australian Aboriginal History: 5 Stories of Indigenous Heroes*. Gold Coast, Qld, The Prison Tree Press.

https://www.jstor.org/stable/j.ctt24hcsc.13?seq=1

Korzelinski, S. (1979) *Memoirs of Gold Digging in Australia*. St Lucia, Qld, University of Queensland Press.

Mahar, C. "Police" https://www.egold.net.au/biogs/EG00187b.htm

Moodie, Georgia (2019) "Coming to terms with the brutal history of Queensland's Native Mounted Police" https://www.abc.net.au/news/2019-07-24/native-mounted-police-indigenous-history-aboriginal-troopers/11296384

National Museum of Australia "NSW Native Police" https://www.nma.gov.au/defining-moments/resources/nsw-native-police

Parry, Naomi (2006) "Musquito (1780–1825)" Australian Dictionary Of Biography http://adb.anu.edu.au/biography/musquito-13124

Pike, G. (1996) *Queensland Frontiers*. Brisbane, Glenville Pike.

Powell, Michael http://www.abc.net.au/news/2016-12-02/musquito-and-tasmanias-black-war/8075714

Richards, Jonathan (2009) "Native Police" https://www.qhatlas.com.au/content/native-police

Richards, Jonathan (2008) *The Secret War: a True History of Queensland's Native Police.* Brisbane, University of Queensland Press

Sovereign Hill
https://sovereignhill.com.au/uploads/resources/SovHill-lawandorder-notes-ss1.pdf

Sovereign Hill Education Blog (2014) "Alcohol on the Goldfields" https://sovereignhilledblog.com/2014/02/21/alcohol-on-the-goldfields/

Sovereign Hill (2014) https://sovereignhilledblog.com/2014/03/20/the-goldfields-police/

Sovereign Hill "Law and Order on the Goldfields" https://sovereignhill.com.au/uploads/resources/SovHill-lawandorder-notes-ss1.pdf

Sovereign Hill "The Native Police" https://sovereignhillhiddenhistories.com.au/gold-commissioners-camp/

SBS https://www.sbs.com.au/gold/lawless-and-disorderly/

State Library of Victoria http://ergo.slv.vic.gov.au/explore-history/golden-victoria/life-fields/law-order

Terra Australis Readers & Writers Festival https://www.terroraustralisfestival.com/mary-cockerill 2021

University of Newcastle (2022) "New evidence reveals Aboriginal massacres committed on extensive scale" https://www.newcastle.edu.au/newsroom/featured/new-evidence-reveals-aboriginal-massacres-committed-on-extensive-scale

Victorian Collections "Many Roads: Stories of the Chinese on the goldfields" https://victoriancollections.net.au/stories/many-roads-stories-of-the-chinese-on-the-goldfields/conflict-harmony

Von Stieglitz, K. R. (2006) "Howe, Michael (1787–1818)"

https://adb.anu.edu.au/biography/howe-michael-2206

Wallis, Lynley, Barker, Bryce, & Burke, Heather (2018) "How unearthing Queensland's 'native police 'camps gives us a window onto colonial violence " https://theconversation.com/how-unearthing-queenslands-native-police-camps-gives-us-a-window-onto-colonial-violence-100814

Washington, Edward https://sydneylivingmuseums.com.au/stories/were-bushrangers-villains-or-heroes

Webber, Kimberley (2001) *Law and Order on the Goldfields.* South Yarra, Vic, Macmillan.

Wise, C. (1983) "Black rebel: Mosquito" pp. 1-7 in E. Fry (ed), *Rebels And Radicals*. Sydney, Allen & Unwin.

# Questions For Further Consideration

How did the gold rushes impact First Nations people?

Why did First Nations people join the Native Police and go against their own people?

Heroes or villains? What do you think about Australian bushrangers?

# About Marji Hill

## Artist & Author

Marji Hill, artist and painter since childhood, runs her art career alongside her career as an author.

Marji is a highly respected international author as well as a seasoned business executive, researcher, and coach.

She is passionate about promoting understanding between Australia's first people and other Australians.

Marji has fostered the spirit of reconciliation in all her writings since she was Research

Fellow in Education at the Australian Institute of Aboriginal and Torres Strait Islander Studies (AIATSIS) in Canberra.

From 2008 to 2011, Marji was Deputy Chairperson of the Mosman Branch of Reconciliation Australia in Sydney.

Following her Education Research Fellowship at AIATSIS in 1976 Marji, together with her late partner, Alex Barlow, produced more than seventy (70) books on all aspects of the First Nations people including the critical, annotated bibliography *Black Australia*.

In 1989 Marji was the Project Coordinator and one of the researchers and writers of *Australian Aboriginal Culture* the official Australian Government publication on First Nations people.

In 1988 her work of non-fiction *Six Australian Battlefields*, which she co-authored with Al Grassby, was published by Angus and Robertson. A decade later it was re-published by Allen & Unwin as a paperback edition.

Her nine-volume encyclopaedia, *Macmillan Encyclopaedia of Australia's Aboriginal Peoples* was published in 2000 and in 2009 she published *The Apology: Saying Sorry To The Stolen Generations.*

Marji's more recent publications extend to self-improvement and self-help with books like *Staying Young Growing Old* and *Inspired by Country* a self-help book about painting with gouache.

Marji's artworks range from very large oil paintings on canvas (her largest being 213 x 167cm) to very small works on paper - gouache being a favourite medium.

Black/white relations, reconciliation, Eureka, and the discovery of gold are common themes not only in her writings but also in her art.

Her small paintings are simple responses to land and sea environments.

Painting has been a lifetime passion for Marji. She remembers as a child winning first prize for a painting she exhibited at the Southport agricultural show. Then in her teens for two years in a row she won the Sunday Mail Child Art Competition in Queensland with her winning paintings getting full coverage in colour in the newspaper.

Marji's formal art training took place in the 1980s at the Canberra School of Art which in 1992 became ANU School of Art & Design.

As soon as she completed her Master of Arts Degree in Anthropology at the Australian National University (ANU), Marji went on to get a Post Graduate Diploma in Painting. She has held eight solo exhibitions in Canberra, Melbourne and Sydney and she has participated in various group shows.

One of her large paintings was included in the 2004- 2005 Art Gallery of Ballarat Travelling Exhibition *Eureka Revisited: the Contest of Memories*. This exhibition travelled to Melbourne, Canberra and Ballarat - part of the 150-year celebration of the Eureka Stockade.

Two of her large paintings were commissioned by the Citigold Corporation. One did hang for many years in the foyer of

Jupiter's Casino in Townsville until the casino was sold, becoming the Ville Resort-Casino.

*Jupiter's Lucky Strike* celebrates the discovery of gold by First Nations boy, Jupiter Mosman in 1871 at Charters Towers in North Queensland. This painting today hangs in the offices of the Citigold Corporation in Charters Towers.

The other, a portrait of Jupiter Mosman resides in the World Theatre in Charters Towers.

Marji's paintings are in many private collections both in Australia and overseas and she is represented in the Art Gallery of Ballarat and the Ballarat and Sydney campuses of the Australian Catholic University.

For many years Marji travelled extensively both within Australia and internationally, working as a consultant, doing speaking engagements, motivating people, and developing her art career.

Marji has returned to her birth place and now resides in Surfers Paradise. She pursues her interests of writing, painting, mentoring, publishing, and internet marketing.

# More Books by Marji Hill

## Self-improvement/Self-Help

Hill, Marji (2014) *Staying Young Growing Old.* Broadbeach, Qld, The Prison Tree Press.

Hill, Marji (2020) *How Big Is Your Why? An Author's Guide to Time Management and Productivity to Achieve Transformational Results.* Broadbeach, Qld, The Prison Tree Press.

Hill, Marji (2020) *A Create and Publish Toolbox: 101 Prompts In A Guided Journal To Help You Write, Self publish, And Market Your Book On Amazon.* Broadbeach, Qld, The Prison Tree Press.

Hill, Marji (2021) *Inspired by Country: an Artist's Journey Back to Nature, Landscape Painting with Gouache.* Broadbeach, Qld, The Prison Tree Press.

# First Nations

Hill, Marji (2021) *First People Then And Now: Introducing Indigenous Australians.* 2nd ed. Broadbeach, Qld, The Prison Tree Press.

Hill, Marji (2021) *Australian Aboriginal History: 5 Stories of Indigenous Heroes.* Broadbeach, Qld, The Prison Tree Press.

# Gold

Hill, Marji (2022) *Gates of Gold: The Discovery of Gold, its Legacy and its Contribution to Australian Identity.* Broadbeach, Qld, The Prison Tree Press.

Hill, Marji (2022) *Shadows of Gold: Eureka and the Birth of Australian Democracy.* Broadbeach, Qld, The Prison Tree Press.

Hill, Marji (2022) *Gold and the Chinese: Racism, Riots and Protest on the Australian*

*Goldfields.* Broadbeach, Qld, The Prison Tree Press.

Hill, Marji (2022) *Ghosts of Gold: The Life and Times of Jupiter Mosman.* Broadbeach, Qld, The Prison Tree Press.

Hill, Marji (2022) *Blood Gold: Native Police, Bushrangers and Law and Order on the Goldfields.* Broadbeach, Qld, The Prison Tree Press.

For a more complete listing of her works, please visit Marji's website:

*https://marjihill.com*

www.ingramcontent.com/pod-product-compliance
Lightning Source LLC
Chambersburg PA
CBHW041459010526
44107CB00044B/1506